Contents

Preface v

Sustainable Deployment of Unutilized Forest Resources in the State of Odisha for Economic Development. 1

1 Brief Constitutional Definition of the Environmental Protection Issues: 4

2 Institutional -*Versus*- Individual Responsibilities of the Public Office Bearers with Defined Duty Assignments: 6

3 The Points of Reference 8

4 An Economic Model of Forestry 11

5 The Economic Cost Burden of the Idle Landscape 15

6 Conceptual Solution to the Problem 17

7 Identifiable Route Cause of the Existing Problem 24

8 Scope of Further Work on the Subject 25

9 Conclusions 27

10 Bibliography 29

Appendix-1: Remote Sensing Imagery Data on Vegetation Mapping ... 30

Appendix-2: Letter to the Government on Forest Fire 32

A CITIZEN'S OPEN LETTER TO HIS
EXCELLENCY THE GOVERNOR OF ODISHA

A
CONCEPT PAPER ON :

SUSTAINABLE DEPLOYMENT OF UNUTILIZED FOREST RESOURCES FOR ECONOMIC DEVELOPMENT

BY PRANAB K. MISHRA

BLUEROSE PUBLISHERS
India | U.K.

Copyright © Pranab K. Mishra 2024

All rights reserved by author. No part of this publication may be reproduced, stored in a retrieval system or transmitted in any form or by any means, electronic, mechanical, photocopying, recording or otherwise, without the prior permission of the author. Although every precaution has been taken to verify the accuracy of the information contained herein, the publisher assumes no responsibility for any errors or omissions. No liability is assumed for damages that may result from the use of information contained within.

BlueRose Publishers takes no responsibility for any damages, losses, or liabilities that may arise from the use or misuse of the information, products, or services provided in this publication.

For permissions requests or inquiries regarding this publication, please contact:

BLUEROSE PUBLISHERS
www.BlueRoseONE.com
info@bluerosepublishers.com
+91 8882 898 898
+4407342408967

ISBN: 978-93-6452-068-3

Cover design: Shivam
Typesetting: Namrata Saini

First Edition: August 2024

Preface

Despite the fact that the state of Odisha is extremely rich in natural resources having 39% of its geographical spread under forest cover, the budgetary data published by the Government[1] shows that the annual revenue earning potential of the forest land in the state is less than Rs.13,000/- per Km^2. For ease of understanding, if we reduce this statistical data into to a daily revenue factor, it comes to around an earning of Rs. 35/- per day per square kilometer. This information reveals that a mere ownership over tangible resources does not make someone resourceful in any literal sense. When this physical resource is not deployed in an effective manner, it remains as a socio-economic burden exerting a heavy charge upon the state exchequer and thus negatively affecting the economic condition of each of its citizens at their respective level. The consequence of the present set of public policy towards the subject for maintaining such a kind and scale of non-performing natural resources is that the committed objectives of the framers of our constitution to improve the overall condition of the citizens, and more particularly those who live in the vicinity of the forests is heavily restrained. Such resources, which should rather be considered as an assets, on the flip side posed itself as a socio-economic liability as it is being perennially subject to forest fire of a devastating scale. The forest dwellers are seemingly trapped in an unescapable geographical prison boundary

---

[1] Annual Financial Statement (2023-24) showing the annual revenue earning of Rs. 78 Cr. from Forestry and Wildlife, out of the 61204 Km^2 of RFA.

along with huge natural resources dumped inside and the grooming unrest amongst them is being leveraged by some organized fractions portraying themselves as subscribers of left-wing ideologies.

Undoubtedly, there are some fundamental shortcomings in the existing public policy from its definition level itself and in its modality of implementation that is responsible for such problems which the Author wants to address through this Concept Paper with some propositions to resolve it. The desired scale of transformation in public policy to make the things right is not considered as possible by the efforts of a single department of the government and hence, it is being addressed to the highest office of His Excellency the Governor of Odisha, in the form of a scholarly concept paper which should not be construed as a representation.

Although the concept paper is state specific, yet the addressed problem and the suggested solutions are universally true for all other states or provinces of India as well.

Sustainable Deployment of Unutilized Forest Resources in the State of Odisha for Economic Development.

CS Pranab K. Mishra[2]

A. **INTRODUCTION:** The Author on a recent occasion drew the attention of the Govt. of Odisha over the issue of spreading forest fire on an extensive scale in the southern districts of the state (a copy has been enclosed at the end of this paper as **Appendix-2** for recapitulation). From the facts as stated therein that addressing letter, it may be understood that the environmental issues have been substantially and undesirably compromised by the state over the past years. While addressing the issue, the Author as a common citizen had reasons to be judgmental on the question of efficacy of the Forest Department in performing its role of environmental protection in respect to containing the forest fire as discussed therein that letter. Understandably, this is considered as mandatory for the government

---

[2] The Author is a Professional Company Secretary as a Fellowship Member of the Institute of Company Secretaries of India (A statutory institute established under a special Act of the Parliament) and formerly he was a gazetted officer in the Union Finance Ministry before he preferred voluntary retirement.

to control such environmental hazards and it is the moral responsibility of the persons in power to fix the problem even in absence of any contemplation from the part of the citizens or interventions from the judicial institutions.

However, in the instant concept paper the Author analyzes the subject of Forestry from the viewpoints of an economist and found that natural resources of an enormous scale have been mistakenly or rather unattentively trapped beneath the government policies and programs related to the subject which could rather be effectively utilized for economic development of the region. The policy propositions through this concept paper may initiate a sustainable economic trajectory promoting economic growth, creating jobs, reducing poverty and improving the overall wellbeing of the population.

B. **SCOPE AND LIMITATIONS OF THIS CONCEPT PAPER:** Exploring the reasons as to what impairs the efficacy of the Forest Department is a subjective issue and as such this concept paper can only marginally define the problem from a limited perspective. With limitations to access to the primary statistical data sources on the subject matter, the Author, despite having a multi-disciplinary academic and professional background and long experience in active government service in his career, views that he could just be able to touch the bottom line of the issue at this stage of analysis. What this paper does not cover is a reference to the basic definition of the problem of environmental hazards and its consequences, considering it a notorious fact known to everyone.

Furthermore, it is to accept that the proposition of any economic model fundamentally subjects to uncertainty at all stages of its lifecycle as it is being guided by human factors since the behavioral pattern of human beings who may influence the model is extremely complicated and erratic. But anyway, that should not restrict us from taking steps to achieve the objectives by accepting those challenges with utmost caution.

1

Brief Constitutional Definition of The Environmental Protection Issues:

The recitation in the Constitution of India (COI) that starts with *"WE THE PEOPLE OF INDIA..."* in its Preamble denotes that each legislation, policy and program pursued by the government ought to be citizen centric by nature. But when the Environmental protection issue as a citizens' right is put forth for a normative examination, it is found that Article 21 of the COI which deals with personal life and liberty issues does not expressly contemplate the same as a distinct and identifiable fundamental right. Rather, the subject has been categorized as a Directive Principle of State Policy u/A. 48A[3] of the COI that makes it optional for the government to pursue the same and hence, somehow diminishes its value in implementation parameters through judicial intervention. In other words, no citizen or private organization in India may legally force the government to pursue an effective environmental policy.

However, in a fundamentally belated move, in 2022, the United Nations General Assembly (UNGA) unanimously recognized the right to access a clean, healthy, and sustainable environment as a human right which altogether altered the world's view on the subject matter. Once it

---

[3] Ins. by the Constitution (Forty-second Amendment) Act, 1976, s. 10 (w.e.f. 3-1-1977).

achieves the status of a human right, its position shifts beyond the surface line of constitutionally declared fundamental rights, and as such it may no longer be considered as a non-obligatory task for a nation state.

Thus, at least in a literary context it may be said that any act of omission[4] or commission by a private or a public person, entity or an institution that leads to infringement or diminishing of collective rights of the mankind on environmental parameters is now conceivably tantamount to a human right violation.

However, the accuracy of the definition as provided by the UNO that influences its effectiveness is subject to scholarly criticisms. Defining an issue whether it is in science or humanities is not an easy task which may be understood from a simple example of Lord Buddha who spent twelve years to simply define the term 'sorrow' in human life. Such a definition as provided by the UNO linking 'environment' to 'human rights' is not absolute and universal because the environmental hazards are not affecting the human beings alone but rather biologically affects the entire lifeform and chemically degrades numerous non-living things on earth. So, the current definition of the UNO is not pervasive, all-encompassing and absolute. As such, the responsibility of the nation states and their policy makers towards the subject should not be limited to the extent with reference to the definition as provided by the UNO. When it is so difficult to provide a definition to the environmental issue, quite understandably it is not an easy task to lay out a schematic relationship between the subject matter and those human factors like the legislative and executive mindset as its affecting corollaries.

---

[4] Sub-sec.(2) to section 3 of the General Clauses Act, 1897 defining the term act as: *"(2) "act", used with reference to an offence or a civil wrong, shall include a series of acts, and words which refer to acts done extend also to illegal omissions."*

2

Institutional -*Versus*- Individual Responsibilities of The Public Office Bearers with Defined Duty Assignments:

The informed citizens, think-tanks and the civil societies worldwide ever cast more reliance on the 'permanent executives' like the secretaries to the government with established academic background in contrast to their elected representatives for many logical reasons. When the subject matter of this paper is being construed as involving a human right issue it casts a moral responsibility upon the relevant departments to take due care of it. Therefore, it is hoped, expected and aspired from the part of the office bearers in the Forest Department that they should be profoundly sensitive and responsive towards their assigned responsibilities in one hand and moral responsibilities in the other even though it is undefined.

At least in such a context, the informed citizens expect that the permanent executives shall not take a resort behind the institutional veil even though they are fairly guarded under the present set-up against official or judicial reprimands for their omissions, commissions and non-attentiveness. From both the sides, i.e. from the end of the Department on one hand and from the citizens on the other, it is expected that some degree of formal or informal participation by outreaching to each other should be there on the issue of policy making and its implementation. It is needless to say that the responsibility of devising such a mechanism is cast upon the Department, or, so to say, on the office bearers in the Department. Hence, a committee may be formed, and the private participants may be carefully selected and adequately incentivized and compensated for the quality time they contribute.

3

The Points of Reference

The Author, being a corporate management professional with his long association with the Union Finance Ministry, has an inclination to begin his study on the departmental inefficacy from the economic facet of the matter. For this purpose, he picked the Annual Financial Statement (2023-24) of the state of Odisha that was prepared by the state's Finance Department and presented before the state legislative assembly. Such a public report typically contains two distinct accounting cross-sections in it viz. the revenue and the expenditure part. The finances of the forest, environment and the ecological heads of account as the same appears in the report have been re-casted below with their interpretation.

i. As the Revenue Accounts Receipts under the Major Budget Head No. 0406, the total annual revenue income for the relevant year from 'Forestry and Wildlife' has been shown therein the report as Rs. 78.00 Crore only.

ii. Whereas, in the expenditure side from the same sector with Major Head 2406, the expenses have been projected as Rs. 1053.00 Crore.

iii. The Capital outlay (Expenses) for the sector is only Rs. 5.00 Crore; and

iv. There was a loan provided to the sector for an amount of Rs.15 Lakh only.
v. Similarly, for Ecology and Environment under the Major Head 3435 there was a budgetary allocation of Rs. 77.00 Crore to meet the expense for the year.

A retrospection over the above abstracts reveals that with a staggering 61,000 Km^2 of officially recorded forest area (RFA) in the state, which is over 39% of the state's entire geographical spread, the above financial statistics showing its revenue earning potential around Rs.13,000/ per Km^2, that looks both meager as well as miserable as it has been viewed below:

a. Revenue from forestry and wildlife merely stands at 0.42% of the total revenue of the state.
b. Expense on forestry and wildlife merely stands at 0.67% of the total expense of the state.
c. However, the most stunning information that is hidden beneath this data cluster is that, the state had a budgetary allocation of 'Rs.77 Crore for Ecology and Environment' in correspondence to the total 'revenue being generated from Forestry and Wildlife that stands at Rs.78 Crore'.

This very information reveals the scope of the state's propensity and preparedness for assuming ecological risk factors. With reference to the above dataset, we may intelligently presume that if there shall be more sectoral revenue generation, the state with the present mindset would not hesitate to allocate a like amount of funds for ecology and environment.

The above interpretation gives rise to a question as to whether there would be a sustainable way to raise revenue from this sector, which matter is being addressed in the following chapters.

4

An Economic Model of Forestry

Here, we may start with the very basic definition of 'Economics' which denotes 'a process of efficient deployment of a scarce resource to yield the best possible alternative result'. So, the standard criterion for taking Economic oriented decisions is having the following notable features:

- There must be an identifiable resource.
- The resource must be scarce and NOT in abundance.
- The resources must have alternate uses.
- There must be feelings of requirement to be fulfilled.
- Devising an intelligent method for best use of the scarce resources.

It is apparent that this basic high school level textbook definition of Economics is seldom being sensibly used by most of us in the real-life scenario as a problem-solving tool. Economic use of something can only be thought out where at the first place the resource is considered as scarce and not abundant and where there is a scope for its alternative use. A classic example illustrating this phenomenon is the position of a sailor in an ocean for whom there is no meaning of 'economic use' of sea water because of its contextual abundance for him.

In the given context we need to identify the 'resource' that is associated with the subject 'Forestry' with reference to the state of Odisha and understand its limits. The official data of the Forest Department says that 39% of the geographical spread of the state is the Recorded Forest Area (RFA) out of which only 3.21% of the total area as per the assessment of the Forest Survey of India[5] is covered with trees. That means only 8% of the RFA is covered with trees and the rest of the 72% of RFA that is under the control of the Forest Department is without trees (which may more rationally be termed as 'a treeless forest'). That 72% of RFA is understandably covered with shrubs, bushes or it is a stony and barren landscape or alike. The inferences drawn by the Author from the above data-analysis are as follows:

- If the Forest Department could effectively double the tree cover area to at least a 6% level of the total geographical area of the state in a strategic manner over a projected period of the next 10-20 years that would be considered as a remarkable achievement for them.
- The contribution of the Forest Department is applaudable for its commendable role as a deterrent to mindless exploitation of forest resources by private individuals, for which at least 3% of the area is maintained as tree bearing forests.
- 72% of the RFA or over 44,000 Km^2 of geographical area i.e. 1,08,72,637 Acres of land which is officially recognized as RFA is not a forest area in any sense.

---

[5] Forest Survey of India Assessment 2021.

- Statistically speaking, it may be reckoned as a per-family[6] stake of 1.1 Acre of land that is improperly classified as such, and every poor family of this state would be questioning over this stake of theirs. It is quite understandable that had they been a little understanding of the subject matter their voice would be louder enough to attract the attention of the legislatures. Hence, the state in general and its office bearers having knowledge and understanding all about the subject matter in particular require having an introspection over the matter as to how this infrastructure resource would be properly engaged and utilized.

- Hence, it seems expedient here for all of us to analyze the subject matter and its implications more from the perspective of an economist at the first place than as an administrator or legislature.

- It is understood that once convinced, the permanent executives in the state may easily and effectively initiate the process of drafting a policy and get the formal consent of the legislatures.

- If we shall try to conceive the statistics of RFA in historical perspectives, we may find that the fact of 3.21% tree coverage of the geographical spread of the state as per the assessment of the Forest Survey of India *ibid* has been cardinally true ever since from the pre-independence era which has not been improved in any way since then despite the best efforts of the forest department made through various sectoral programs like the mass plantation drives and social forestry. The above analysis has been made on the basis

---

[6] Considering around 96.5 Lakh families residing in the state of Odisha as per the 2011 census.

of the data populated from the official website of the forest department of Odisha as presented below:

"On 1 April 1936, Odisha emerged as a new state of India; and a new Forest Department was formed under the charge of a Conservator of Forests. The Madras Presidency, Central Provinces as well as old Bihar and Odisha contributed equally to areas of forests and the total area of reserved forests and demarcated forest stood at 1401 and 583 sq. miles respectively."[7]

On the basis of the above statistical data, we may make the following calculation and draw our inferences:

- $1401 + 583 = 1984$ mile^2 :: 5139 Km^2 which is roughly 3.29% of the total geographical area of the state (that comprises of 155707 Km^2) was the extent of designated reserve forest of that historical time.

- As such, inferences may be drawn that there has been no increase in the forest area since then. Thus, the term 'RFA' is a misnomer being deployed for classification of forest areas in the state which actually represents the residual idle land mass to a huge extent up to 39% (including 3.29% actual forest area) that is numerically inflated to over 10 times of the actual forest covered area in the state.

Such a misclassification has far reached negative implications on the economics of the state as has been discussed in the following chapters.

---

[7] Web source: https://odishaforest.in/about-us/History-Evolution, version. 6th of June 2024.

5

The Economic Cost Burden of the Idle Landscape

There is an important 'cost factor' defined in Cost Accounting which is termed as 'Opportunity Cost'. Theoretically, if a particular resource has possible alternative uses, the intrinsic notional value of that resource is to be recognized and deducted as a charge on its revenue earning potential.

A classic example of opportunity cost is that: if a person is having a scope of running a tea stall in his village and he has a prospect of earning Rs. 100/- per day sitting in his village itself he may never aspire to move to the state capital to work as an NMR[8] for a wage of 200 rupees if he requires to spend over 100 rupees to meet his daily expenses to stay at his workplace. He would rather prefer to stay home even if he does not instantly consider jumping into the said business. However, such a condition of idleness exerts an intrinsic and notional cost burden upon his family up to the extent of the opportunity cost of his prospective income from a tea stall. Similarly, the cost of viewing a TV serial may be

---

[8] The term NMR (Nominal Muster Roll) stands for a contingent worker who is normally paid on a daily basis and hence, not considered as an employee of an organization.

reckoned circumstantially by taking into consideration the scope of alternate productive engagement of that time by that individual viewer.

With such established costing tools in hand, it is possible that the recurring notional 'opportunity cost' burden of the idle or non-performing RFA (hereinafter referred to as the NP-RFA) on the public exchequer of the state may be statistically reckoned with utmost arithmetical nicety. However, rationally it may be construed that it is a substantial amount which might be effectively catered, capitalized through transforming into revenue, and deployed for amelioration of the economic condition of the state.

6

Conceptual Solution to the Problem

Once the problem is recognized and a proper definition for it is laid down after understanding its inherent factors, exploring a solution to the problem may be easier to plan out.

The identifiable task before us now is to prepare a program to deploy the maximum possible extent of the NP-RFA into productive use. Drafting the implementation modality of such a concept may be a little bit harder which would require a coordinated effort from the part of the technical experts from the forest, revenue, finance, law and other departments.

It is visualized in the given context that: simply through scientific farming of fruit and vegetable plants of high yield verities, the NP-RFA may sustainably and economically be converted into a well performing eco-system which is the central theme of this Concept Paper. By that way even those areas shall lose their so called RFA status but from environmental viewpoints those modified farmlands would maintain or even supplementally contribute to the ecology in exceeding the current contribution level of the sporadic and inconsistent canopy of bushes and shrubs they bear. In simple terms, the modality factors of the concept are as follows:

- To identify the NP-RFA areas which could be converted into horticultural farms.

- To gather the data of existing initiatives of the Government and private individuals in cashew, bamboo or coffee plantation in a similar mode and run a SWOT[9] analysis to understand the intricacies in the prospective projects.

- To adopt a CBA[10] to aid the decision-making process for sacrificing the existing status of the RFA. It should be done by keeping in view all the visible parameters, challenges, notional costs, prospects and consequences etc.

- Set the modality of its conversion viz. granting the lands for long-term lease to private participants with defined norms of responsibilities and obligations, exploring for a PPP mode or the scope of doing it through a public institution through contractors or otherwise in a BOT[11] mode.

Out of the above stated modalities as may be proposed for implementation of a massive RFA conversion project, the most unconventional and controversial one is to think about extending the infrastructure on a long term lease basis in favor of private investors. The Author has carefully chosen this model for a brief discussion here in this Concept Paper.

---

[9] The term denotes to: strengths, weaknesses, opportunities, and threats, which is a popular management tool to assess effectiveness of business models before inception.

[10] Cost Benefit Analysis as a management tool.

[11] Build-operate-transfer mode.

Being a socialist republic, so far on every occasion the policymakers of our nation exhibit a habitual propensity to put the interest of the most disadvantaged class of citizens at the foremost agenda in all government programs. At the very second place they want to keep the stake of the government in a commercial project to the utmost level and hence prefer to float PSUs or Cooperatives to keep those projects under the active and absolute control of the government.

However, we all have some or other skeptical opinion over the issue as to how and why the performance of the government projects does not live up to the expectations of anyone. Therefore, at least this time we should begin the other way around by favoring a capitalistic and market-driven model of the project with the following straight forward policy attributes:

- In the first phase the state may think of offering patches of lands to private individuals to occupy and develop horticulture farms in designated areas.
- The allotted pieces of land should be large enough to make the individual projects commercially viable.
- Government servants should be encouraged to participate in the acquisition through their family members. In fact, there is an inner urge in everyone to acquire a farmhouse, that emanates from a natural instinct to create and care for something that responds, even though it is a plant or an animal (preferably not a human being). If it shall be facilitated by the government in this way both the private participants as well as the government servants' families shall intend to invest in it that would consequently contribute to the overall economic progress of the region.

- The existing large trees in the allotted area should be maintained and even the smaller bushes should not altogether be spared or removed at once but provisioned to stay alongside in a controlled manner with the plantation until the valuable plants fully grow and take over the vegetation coverage level of the area to its utmost extent.

- Remote Sensing Satellite imagery system should be put in use for monitoring the overall status of the wild as well as planted vegetation in the farming areas and its real time ecological health rating should be perpetually published on a unified portal with automated algorithm-based advisories for rectification and remedies for the signs of scored degradations of vegetation in the deployed areas.

- The lease rent should be carefully designed with floating charges linked to the standard yielding parameters to support the feasibility of the prospective project proposition and to encourage the investors.

- The valuation may be made for the progressive transformation stage and there should be flexibility for the lessees to convey stake by selling out to other prospective buyers at any stage for a fair value. So, liquidity shall increase its value in the marketplace.

- Because the horticultural projects are labor intensive in nature it shall provide a fair opportunity to the local tribal community to contribute manpower and consequently improve their integration with the outsider world. It shall increase the production of foodstuffs for domestic consumption with export potential as well. Food processing units shall thrive in the area by catering to the central subsidy schemes that may increase the employment opportunities in the area. Amongst many other options, with today's technology, poly-ponds may be cheaply created by deploying earthmovers and drip irrigation systems backed by solar power units can be installed at any remote location. Mixed farming may be practiced with the help of the fishery and animal husbandry departments by which the commercial viability of such farms may be achieved and its breakeven may be lowered.

- It is noteworthy to mention here that during the recent decades the European investors ventured into the deserts of the Middle East and established date palm farms in gigantic scale and similarly in the Asia-pacific region of Indonesia and Malaysia in our very neighborhood they initiated and established commercial scale palm oil farms. Learning from their experience, after keeping the provisions of an additional 3-10% land out of the RFA (out of 39% in official records) to achieve the target for tree plantation to double the existing level of tree coverage as discussed supra, the rest of the landform may be phased out of their RFA status and deployed for sustainable horticultural farming. By that way the program for tree plantation to increase the forest as being pursued by the forest department may become more focused, targeted and result oriented.

- On the other hand, a criticism may crop up that such an allotment system may consequent upon fostering economic inequality in the society as the allottees as a small group of individuals shall get benefits out of it. However, in the views of the Author, undeniably such a situation shall arise at micro-economic level. But at the macro-economic parameters the proposition shall lead to an overall economic progress, and the disparity shall be within the scope of that bracketed growth parameters and not in any way lead to improper distribution of the existing resources. With overall growth rate and the overall employment generation potential, this policy proposition shall yield net positive results and not net negative results. Hence, such small problems may be intelligently ignored for a greater cause.

It is quite pertinent here to draw some inferences out of the fact of British colonial legacy and its nexus with the private land ownership rights and its corollary influencing the current GDP[12] of different modern states as below:

1. Once a British Colony and its economy principally founded upon distributed private land ownership rights, the per capita GDP of USA today stands at $ 76,330 that is a staggering 32 times of India's GDP (PC) which meagerly stands at $2,411 per annum.
2. Similarly, Austrillia and Canada both of which still consider themselves as British colonies are having annual GDP(PC) of $65,100 and $55,522 i.e. 27 and 23 times that of India respectively.

The Peoples Republic of China has been extensively pursuing a systematic national policy of allotting lands in favor of its citizens in the country sides for their use without extending ownership rights, which has proved successful in ameliorating poverty and increasing the national income.[13]

---

[12] Web reference data for 2022:
https://data.worldbank.org/indicator/NY.GDP.PCAP.CD

[13] Web reference: http://www.npc.gov.cn/zgrdw/englishnpc/Law/2007-12/12/content_1383939.htm

The above information compels us to rethink about the policy of vesting of the residual land ownership rights with the state that has understandably been covered under a pseudo definition of RFA and it defies the public attention. It may be imagined as to how the socio-economic condition of the state shall transform if each of its family would be offered an acre of land for use in their own way even without transferring ownership rights in their favor. Distribution of resources amongst the citizens is an important task of the nation and by reserving such a huge resource under the definition of RFA we have lost the scope for its proper utilization in proper time.

7

Identifiable Route Cause of the Existing Problem

Whether it is an academics, management, commerce or public administration sector, everywhere we feel the pervasiveness of a 'classification' and 'definition' clause. Here in this paper the term RFA has been extensively discussed. This innocent looking acronym is not merely a term by itself, but it encompasses a whole gamut of expressed and implied objectives, obligations or limitations for both the government and for the public, and it is a source of authority for the department which may be used or misused. Once the term is created and its meaning consolidated it fosters a deeply rudimentary sense and everyone seemingly wants to take resort to it to justify the inertia that allows no progress or dynamism in the sector. A scholarly anatomy of this term is felt to be very much essential to fixing the problems in the given sector that is consequent upon the criticalities arising out of the definition and its corollaries.

8

Scope of Further Work on the Subject

As it has already been discussed, the data available with the department of forest is to be gathered and a few additional field level information may be collected through normal official channels. Similar project initiatives which are already in place may be studied and the data about the practical experience of the staff in the sector as populated may be reduced to actionable information. The problems in the constitution and operation of state-run cooperatives and PSUs in similar commercial ventures may be keenly studied to understand the effectiveness of such management systems in the proposed enterprise. For this purpose, there is a need to create a well drafted questionnaire booklet through which not only the relevant data, but also the opinion of different offices and stakeholders may be collected.

More importantly, while planning for such changes, there is a need to escape from the mental inertia that crystalized ever since the British promulgated the Forest Act of 1865 followed by a National Forest Policy of 1894 defining the goal of their Crown on the subject matter the essence of which is still being felt in the present form of the forest law in operation. The fundamental nature of the statutes is such that it develops a propensity and mental inclination of everyone towards adhering to the existing position of laws and seldom or rarely people think about changing their approach towards the subject when it is once settled or declared by the sovereign as a policy. However, there is a necessity to put flexible legislative approach towards the statutes and policies which should be constantly analyzed and dynamically changed to synchronize with the changing goals of society. It should not be though that once a law or a policy is made it is made for ever as the colonial form of law has ever trained our minds.

9

Conclusions

It is not an uncommon world phenomenon that many nations with rich natural resources as well as vast geographical area perennially remain poor and they confer upon their citizens a kind of destituted living condition in contrast to some nation states like that of Japan with inadequate natural resources but still ensuring higher GDP, higher growth rate, higher living standards and higher per capita income for their citizens. The farmers of the public policies in our nation, with good reasons, seem to have ever been relying on several borrowed phenomenon which are successfully implemented in different parts of the world in different times.

At the outset it may is realizable that a major portion of our Constitution have been straightly borrowed from other nations. Similarly, the concepts of land ceiling, five-year plans, green revolution, industrial parks, SEZs, smart cities and many more have been borrowed from others. There is *per se* no harm in borrowing the established and time-tested concepts from others, but it is a matter of concern that almost every time we failed to achieve the desired results or the desired level of results because of the incompatibility factors in such programs to the prevailing domestic context which could not be properly considered while adopting those concepts.

At least this time, the Author has an opinion that we must plan for a zero-based projecting formula for policy making in the proposed sector by taking into reference all the contextual parameters populated from original sources because we may not find a ready-made project of this kind anywhere else in the world.

After carefully drafting of the policy and setting out its modalities for implementation it is needless to conclude about the end results of such an initiative.

10

Bibliography

1. Remote sensing imagery in vegetation mapping: a review, Yichun Xie and others *Journal of Plant Ecology*, Volume-1, March 2008, Oxford University Press, web reference: www.jpe.oxfordjournals.org.

2. The Constitution of India.

3. Basic Economics, Thomas Sowell.

4. Good Economics for Hard Times, Abhijit V. Banerjee.

5. China's Economy, Arthur R Kroeber.

6. Forest Administration in South Odisha under the British Raj (A.D. 1858-1947) A Study, Pramila Khadanga.

Appendix-1

Remote Sensing Imagery DATA on Vegetation Mapping

For the policy making process, extensive data on the relevant subject is required which may be obtained from remote sensing satellite sources. It is important to keep in mind that the proposed policy shall result in massive alteration in vegetation composition in a significantly large area eliminating the natural mixed vegetation types by substituting the same with organized vegetation types. The ecological impact of such modifications is to be predicted. Secondly, the decision about deployment of patches of landscape may be taken after a thorough feasibility analysis based on remote sensing data that provides information about distribution of ground water level and the soil types. The traditional method of field survey, literature review or study of the maps by the agencies or by the relevant government departments has its own limitations and hence the remote sensing data is to be deployed for formulation of the policy in an effective, time bound and cost-effective manner. However, the traditional methods are to be deployed alongside for achieving better results.

There are several international remote sensing satellites viz. Landsat (mainly TM and ETM+), SPOT, MODIS, NOAA–AVHRR, IKONOS and QuickBird and around 33 numbers of Indian remote sensing satellites including the IRS, EOS and Cartosat series which have scanned and gathered data of the earth's surface during their operational life period[14]. The onboard sensors of such satellites have improved extensively ever since their initial deployment in the early 1970s.

High resolution Ground Sampling Distance (GSD) as low as 0.5m is achievable today with the latest sensors onboard. Further, the available technology identifies the communities (group of all kinds of vegetation in a sample area) or species (individual kind of plants) level vegetation types. A scholarly article titled 'Remote sensing imagery in vegetation mapping: a review' by Yichun Xie and others published in the *Journal of Plant Ecology, Volume-1* of March 2008 that is available online at www.jpe.oxfordjournals.org provides important information about the specific subject matter which may be studied for getting broader ides on the subject. The Regional Remote Sensing Centre of ISRO, for the eastern region is situated in Kolkata, West Bengal that serves the state of Odisha which may provide important information on the subject and coordinate with the Government of Odisha to design the plan for the project and monitor its implementation steps.

---

[14] https://www.isro.gov.in/Indian_Remote_Sensing_Satellite_1A.html

Appendix-2

Letter to the Government on Forest Fire

From:
CS Pranab Kumar Mishra
207, Rajarani Towers,
Komapalli, Berhampur, Dt. Ganjam
9438413005 / 8658614116
pranab.kmp@gmail.com

To: His Excellency the Governor of Odisha

(THROUGH SHRI SASWAT MISHRA, IAS PRINCIPAL SECRETARY TO THE GOVERNOR)

Sub: A Citizen's report about an extensive scale of forest fire in southern districts of Odisha requiring urgent state action.

[When the Departments seems to be dysfunctional on an emergency situation it is felt expedient to alert the highest office of the state]

Hon'ble Governor Sir,

This is to report to your Excellency about the event of sporadic breakout of forest fire of extensive scale in the southern districts of the state, and it is apparent that the branches of the state administration upon which the responsibility to contain the fire is entrusted are not effectively doing anything in that direction. This fact came to the knowledge of the undersigned when he was on a trip to Jeypore (Koraput District) from Berhampur (Ganjam District) between 5th to 7th of this month of April,2024. A few images of the incident taken at different locations have been enclosed those define the gravity of the situation. At many places, as it may be seen from the images that the entire flora of the terrains is annihilated. Over scores of miles on the road the air is potentially thick, smokey and hot and its consequences may be well conceived.

In a similar context, when such incidents occur in other parts of the globe, we witness swift and serious approach from the part of the administration of those countries but here, there is no visible action being taken by the forest or the district authorities to address the situation.

The undersigned explored the state policies and found that a statute namely the Orissa Forest (Fire Protection) Rules, 1979 backed by a well-defined SOP is rightly at its place that suggests a coordinated role of the District Administration and the Forest Department to control the forest fire. But it is quite apparent that the initial parameters of populating relevant information and its official reporting are not being observed by them for which the matter is seemingly left unreported to the departmental headquarters at the state capital.

However, the author has shared the satellite images at the end of this document as populated from NASA's Fire Information and Resource Management System (FIRMS) which shows that the fire has been intensified to this scale only since 27th of March 2024. The Forest and Environment Department HQ might have used the data and raised an alarm to the field staff to take possible measures. With such a level of information technology at place, there is no necessity to depend on the traditional statistical data from the ground staff. Further, the typical official approach of disaster management may be altogether converted to a top-down one wherein the primary data shall be populated by the HQs itself wherever it is possible.

One of the probable reasons for such underreporting of information is because the relevant departments would be taking such events into granted as a regular occurrence. In absence of conscious reports of this mishap on media or from the civil societies, everyone might be considering it as a natural phenomenon; for which the officers also would be mentally indifferent towards it. The District Administration with a DM as a quite a junior cadre officer would be silent by holding individual perceptions that it is unnecessary to alert the Government, which would rather be detrimental to his position. Conceivably, it is an information and statistical blackout by the field formation for which the 'program' as per the defined 'policy' of the state is not being effectively implemented.

Definitely, when the house is factually on fire it would not be considered as an appropriate time for mind storming over its causes like the human factor involved in it or about its long-term solutions. Hopefully, your excellency shall take the matter seriously and direct the concerned departments to do the needful to control this environmental hazard.

Yours sincerely,

Place: Berhampur
Date: 9th of April 2024

CS Pranab Kumar Mishra

NASA's (FIRMS) IMAGES

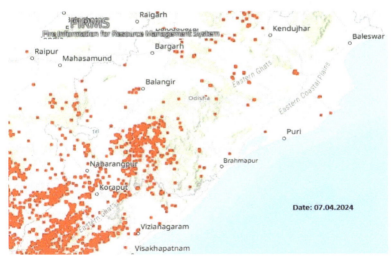

Milton Keynes UK
Ingram Content Group UK Ltd.
UKHW052342221024
450028UK00027B/269